NORTH LIGHT
GRAPHIC WORKBOOKS

Marker Techniques

FOOD
WORKBOOK 7

Lee Woolery

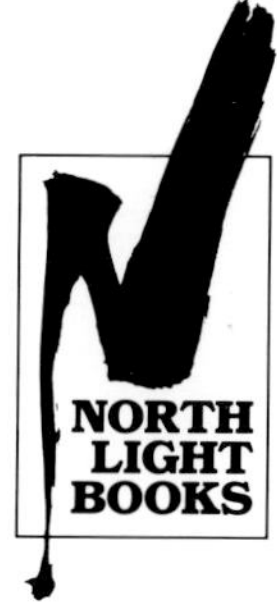

NORTH
LIGHT
BOOKS

Cincinnati, Ohio

ISBN 0-89134-275-3

Concept and editorial development by
Diana Martin
Interior design by Carol Buchanan

INTRODUCTION

Food renderings must look good enough to eat. Fresh, clean color characterizes a successful marker rendering of food. Unlike some subjects, food leaves no leeway for depicting tones; the color must glow and create a mouth-watering look. A food rendering must convince its viewer to purchase the product. Your subject must look as if it was just picked or fresh from the oven.

As you might imagine, food is one of the most difficult subjects to render in marker. No client will accept an unappetizing rendering, one that shows his product in a poor light. Yet food rendering is worth the challenge since it can offer you a myriad of graphic art opportunities. Television commercials, for example, must be rendered in marker form before they are filmed, and food companies, as you've undoubtedly noticed, make extensive use of TV advertising. Food renderings are used in many other areas of the professional world. Since grocery stores advertise in newspapers, clean marker indications are necessary in designing layouts. Package designs also make use of renderings for comps and mock-ups. Fast-food chains are always introducing new products, and marker renderings are needed in their promotion. Clearly, your opportunities are limited only by the marker skills you possess.

The Series

To complete this workbook, the seventh in the series *Marker Techniques,* it's essential that you know the principles and skills taught in the first six workbooks. By this time, you should have enough experience in marker rendering to successfully tackle food products.

If you feel at all unsure about any marker rendering technique, go back to the earlier workbooks and refresh your memory. In order to complete the projects in this workbook, you must understand the terminology and have a mastery of the techniques taught by the preceding books. If you

This comp demonstrates one of the most important characteristics of any food rendering—fresh, clean, vibrant color, which results in appetizing food.

haven't completed an earlier workbook, do so before proceeding any further with this book.

As in the previous workbooks, in this one you'll continue to *participate.* The projects feature step-by-step demonstrations and instructional captions that show you the mechanics of each technique, as

well as the way different rendering methods can be combined. A full-page reproduction of each finished image follows the last project. After you've studied the how-tos of each project, turn to the practice pages following the last demonstration and begin!

Even in this quick layout, it's easy to identify each food product because of their unique surface textures and individual shapes.

Rendering Food

Every food has an individual surface texture that must be rendered accurately. As you develop a food rendering, make sure your marker strokes are not connoting a texture foreign to that particular food. A banana's skin is quite different from that of a squash, although both are yellow on the surface.

When drawing food, you must pay close attention to detail. Some fast foods, for instance, have sesame seeds or special sauces that distinguish them from other brands, and you must be able to indicate that difference. Study a food product's textures and overall shape before putting pen to paper. A 5x0 Rapidograph may be necessary to denote the finer details. You might also want to use colored, fine-line pens for your base drawing, since these lines will disappear as complementary marker colors are applied.

This workbook offers you three food challenges: a chocolate sundae, a sandwich platter, and a ham dish. Each asks you to solve the type of rendering problems that typically face any professional graphic artist.

With the chocolate sundae, your first project, the problem is trying to create a sense of reflective, transparent glass while also showing a tantalizing treat of ice cream, chocolate, and whipped cream. You must make the viewer want to run right out and buy one. Unfortunately, it's very easy to make the glass look like metal, the chocolate look like mud, the whipped cream like cement, and the cherry like it has been out in the sun all day. The key to success—in this and all food renderings—is to build up colors slowly, using the right colors the right way.

Successfully capturing several different types of food is the problem inherent with your second project, the sandwich platter. You have to keep the French fries from looking like wood sticks, the bun from seeming burned, and the chicken patty from resembling pigskin. Again, the key lies in gradually building up your textures and tones. This exercise will teach you how to have patience in developing your renderings.

Meat is probably the hardest substance to render in marker, although the ham featured in your third project is fairly easy compared to steaks, hamburger, or roasts. Ham is pinkish and has brown only on its skin. Beef, on the other hand, is red to reddish brown and can easily look bloody, burned, or rotten if the color is off.

Whenever rendering meat in marker, always simplify your line drawing. Leave out the details or wrinkles that make it unattractive. Trim off the fat and make a pleasant exterior shape, even if your reference doesn't appear that way.

Illustrating with Markers

Since the marker allows a graphic artist to quickly indicate realistic images in black and white or color, it is an invaluable tool whether you work for an advertising agency, a commercial art studio, or an industrial design firm. While marker renderings will never be hung in a museum, they serve a unique purpose in the professional world. Marker is used in storyboards, product design, architectural rendering, layouts, and photo indications. Just as there are several ways in which marker renderings are used—storyboards, product design, and architectural rendering—there are different levels of finish, depending upon the job.

A *thumbnail* is a quick color study that the artist will use to check for balance or composition. Different color combinations can be tried. This rendering is seldom shown to the client.

Layouts are marker indications that are tight enough to show a client but not as time consuming as a comp. Layouts can show how a job will be painted or how it will be photographed. Some mixed media, such as colored pencil or airbrush, may be added.

A *comp* is a rendering that shows beforehand how a printed piece will look. This is usually a tight marker-and-mixed-media representation that looks like final art.

When rendering beef, it's important to keep your colors red to reddish brown so it will look fresh and cooked appropriately for the situation.

As a rule, keep the color toward the pinkish reds or browns and *slowly* build up the intensity. Start with the lightest yellows and pinks to serve as a base tone for unifying the color. To avoid overworking, keep painted highlights to a minimum.

Before you embark on these projects, here are some helpful food rendering guidelines:

1. Make sure all vegetable renderings retain a fresh, just-picked look.
2. Fruits should be rendered with bright, clean colors and crisp highlights.
3. Meats are best indicated with pinks, reds, or reddish browns and never greenish browns.
4. Painted highlights can look like fungus if not properly applied.
5. Greenery or leaves should never be rendered with brownish green markers.
6. Slowly build the markers in layers, paying close attention to the first layers.

Developing Your Own Renderings

At this point, you should have all of the marker techniques' technical problems under control and should be concerning yourself with the more creative aspects of this medium. If you haven't done so already, this is a good time to begin investigating different types of markers and marker paper in anticipation of developing your own renderings.

Throughout this workbook series, I have recommended Berol Prismacolor markers. These alcohol-based markers allow you to glaze as you would with acrylic paints, plus they have a nib at either end. Having a broad nib and a fine point on the same marker not only saves you money, it also makes your working life much simpler.

In addition to alcohol-based markers, you might want to try those with water-soluble pigments. Schwan, Niji, Tombo, Pentel, and Marvy Marker all manufacture quality water-soluble markers in different point sizes. This type of marker is best used for base drawings, since the pigment doesn't bleed when alcohol or solvent-based markers are applied over it. A fine-point is best for drawing, since the ink will dry very quickly, keeping the line from bleeding on the page. Broad-nibbed, water-soluble markers can be used for detail work applied over other pigments. The texture of this pigment will not disturb an illustration's pre-existing color or tear up your paper.

Solvent-based markers are the most popular because so many companies market them. Designer Marker and Chartpak are two of the best-known brands. Solvent markers blend very well, but you must learn to control the bleed. Another drawback is their strong odor, which can make you dizzy and nauseated, especially in a closed room.

If you've chosen a specific marker that you enjoy working with, you may still be casting around for the right paper. Fortunately, you'll find several brands of paper available in well-stocked art supply stores.

Some of the popular brands are Ad-Art, Graphics, Ermine White, Paxton bond, Hammermill Layout bond, and Aquabee 633. These papers vary as to price, amount of bleed, surface, weight, and color fidelity. Ask for samples of the various brands and do your own tests.

All projects in this workbook series were rendered on Aquabee 633. For my needs, this paper offers the right balance of bleed control, color fidelity, and texture. Choice of a marker paper should be based on personal experimentation and not on advice of art supply salespersons. I tried every brand available before finding the one that worked best for me.

Supplies You'll Need

To complete the projects in this workbook, you'll need:

Markers: Berol Prismacolor markers (or a comparable brand) in these colors: cool gray in 30%, 50%, and 80%; warm gray in 10%, 20%, 30%, 40%, 60%, and 80%; ivory, cream, sand; process yellow, cadmium yellow, yellow ochre, orange; blush, light flesh, Apple Blossom, Lipstick Red, brick red, cranberry, vermilion; violet; non-photo blue, light blue, Indigo blue; Grass Green, April Green, Apple Green, dark green; caramel, light tan, dark tan, sienna brown, dark brown, burnt umber; and black.

Other Materials: Dr. Martin's (or a comparable brand) bleedproof white paint; No. 4 sable brush.

RENDERING A CHOCOLATE SUNDAE

 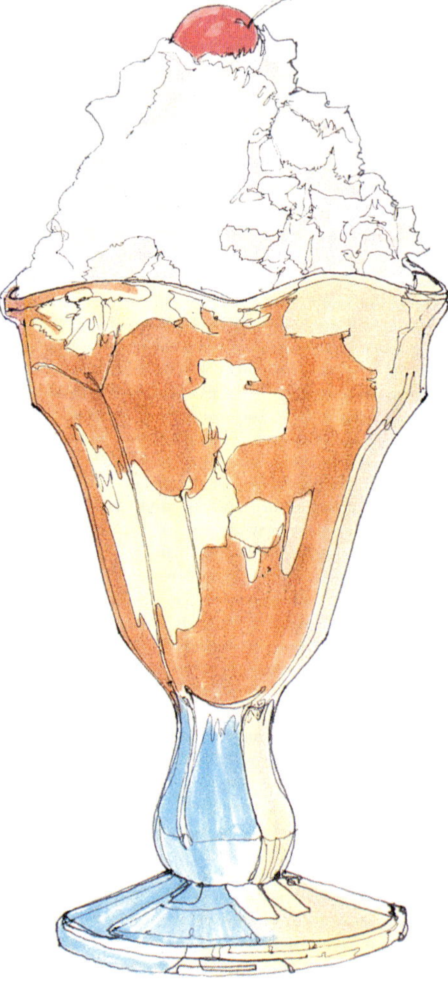 

Step 1: 1) You want the ice cream, the chocolate sauce, and the whipped cream to have a fresh, appealing look. To achieve this effect, you must build up subtle colors slowly, using the fine points of your markers. First, put a layer of Apple Blossom on the cherry. 2) To create the ice cream's base color, apply cream to the entire body of the glass and along the right side of the stem. 3) Next, lightly streak the bottom left side of the stem with non-photo blue.

Step 2: 1) Cover the cherry with Lipstick Red, allowing some of the Apple Blossom to show through as a highlight. 2) Using the drawing's guidelines, carefully fill in the shadows on the whipped cream with 20% warm gray. 3) Following the guidelines for the chocolate sauce, apply vertical strokes of light tan.

Step 3: 1) Dot in the ridged, whipped-cream pattern, using the point of a 10% warm gray marker. 2) Using the guidelines, stroke 50% cool gray below the center of the stem and along the dish's top rim. 3) Dark reflections are indicated at the top of the stem, the dish's top left side, and around the front and bottom edge of the lip with 80% cool gray. 4) Further deepen the chocolate by placing a layer of sienna brown over the light tan. Use this color to draw a reflection in the left side of the dish stand, from the lip at the stem's bottom. 5) Use dark brown to fill in reflections along both sides of the dish and around the top rim.

Step 4: 1) To create more dimension on the whipped cream, dot in 40% warm gray along the ridges and over the 20% gray on the shaded side. 2) Lay dark tan over the chocolate to the right of the dish's middle to give some depth to the shaded side of the glass. 3) Carefully lay in the background with violet. 4) With a No. 4 brush and Dr. Martin's bleedproof white paint, apply shiny white highlights to the cherry, along the left edge of the dish, down the stem, and onto the lip. Next, paint highlights down the middle of the dish and to the left of center.

Step 5: 1) To deepen the value of the chocolate, thereby creating more dimension, carefully add vertical strokes of burnt umber to the sauce area. Be sure to stay within the lines. 2) Finish by neutralizing the intensity of the blue on the dish stem. Glaze over that color with 40% warm gray.

RENDERING A SANDWICH PLATTER

Step 1: 1) The golden tones of the French fries, bun, and chicken patty begin with a yellow tint that is gradually built up into deeper, more intense browns. (Since these objects are rather small, you'll be working again with fine-point markers, unless otherwise noted.) Using strokes that follow the line of each item, apply a cream base over all the food except the salad. 2) Carefully fill in the plate with 10% warm gray. Use loose horizontal strokes, but be sure that this tone doesn't bleed into the cream.

Step 2: 1) With the fine point of a light blue marker, draw a ring on the outside of the plate, then one on the inside around the food. 2) Stroke cadmium yellow over the French fries. 3) Stroke Apple Green over the lettuce. 4) Begin developing the chicken patty's texture with yellow ochre. Using somewhat bumpy strokes, try to replicate a breaded surface, which is darker in some spots and lighter in others. Allow bits of the cream base to show through.

Step 3: 1) Add Lipstick Red to the to-mato and to the apple salad, staying within the guidelines. Use light pres-sure to reduce bleeding. 2) Layer ivory over the bun, working around the ses-ame seeds. The seeds will remain cream colored. 3) Fill in the shadows cast from the food onto the plate, us-ing 30% warm gray. As you draw these shadow reflections with a fine-point, allow some of the undertone to show through. 4) Color the shaded side of each French fry with a sand marker. 5) Cover the pickle with a Grass Green, leaving the highlight un-covered.

Step 4: 1) To create depth on the chicken patty, fill in the edge and the shadow from the bun with light tan. 2) Next, apply brick red around the side of the tomato and along apple bits in the salad. 3) Indicate the texture of lettuce by drawing in wrinkles with a Grass Green marker. 4) Deepen the shadows around the sandwich, the pickle, and the salad, using 60% warm gray. 5) Without touching the sesame seeds, fill in the bun with cadmium yellow.

Step 5: 1) To create roundness and texture, dot yellow ochre around the bun's center, leaving the sesame seeds untouched. 2) Deepen the bun shadow cast on the patty with dark tan. 3) Draw a cranberry shadow along the area where the meat touches the tomato. 4) To add more dimension to the French fries, dot yellow ochre along the shaded side. 5) Darken the shadows around the sandwich and the pickle, using 80% warm gray. 6) Using a combination of vertical and horizontal strokes, fill in the background with sienna brown. Use the broad nib. To avoid bleeding on the sandwich or plate, start by outlining the objects, then work into the larger areas. Once that color dries, apply a layer of dark brown, using the broad nib. Make these strokes bold. They'll add liveliness to the background while drawing attention to the central subject.

RENDERING A HAM

Step 1: 1) Although meat is probably the most difficult food to render successfully in marker, the techniques taught throughout this series should give you satisfactory results. Unless otherwise noted, render each step in fine-point. Begin by applying cream to the ham's outside skin, all of the fruits, and the green garnish. This hue will keep all of the other colors fresh. 2) Apply a layer of light flesh to the inside of the meat, leaving the edges and the middle bone white. 3) Give the silverware a base tone of 20% warm gray.

Step 2: 1) Stroke a smooth layer of caramel over the ham's skin and the skin on the two slices lying on the plate. With a light, ruffling motion, color the parsley April Green. 2) Give the fruits a coat of process yellow. Add more color to the meat by loosely filling in blush. Use a stroking motion that connotes the texture of ham, leaving the bones and some of the fat white. 3) To show dimension on the silverware, carefully draw in the shaded side, using 40% warm gray. Indicate darkness below the platter with 30% cool gray. 4) Continue to refine the meat, using a layer of cream. Also stroke this color over the bones and fat. While the cream layer is still wet, add a layer of light flesh *to the meat only.* 5) Following the guidelines, indicate the cross-cut pattern on the skin with sienna brown. Use this color also to darken the right side of the ham.

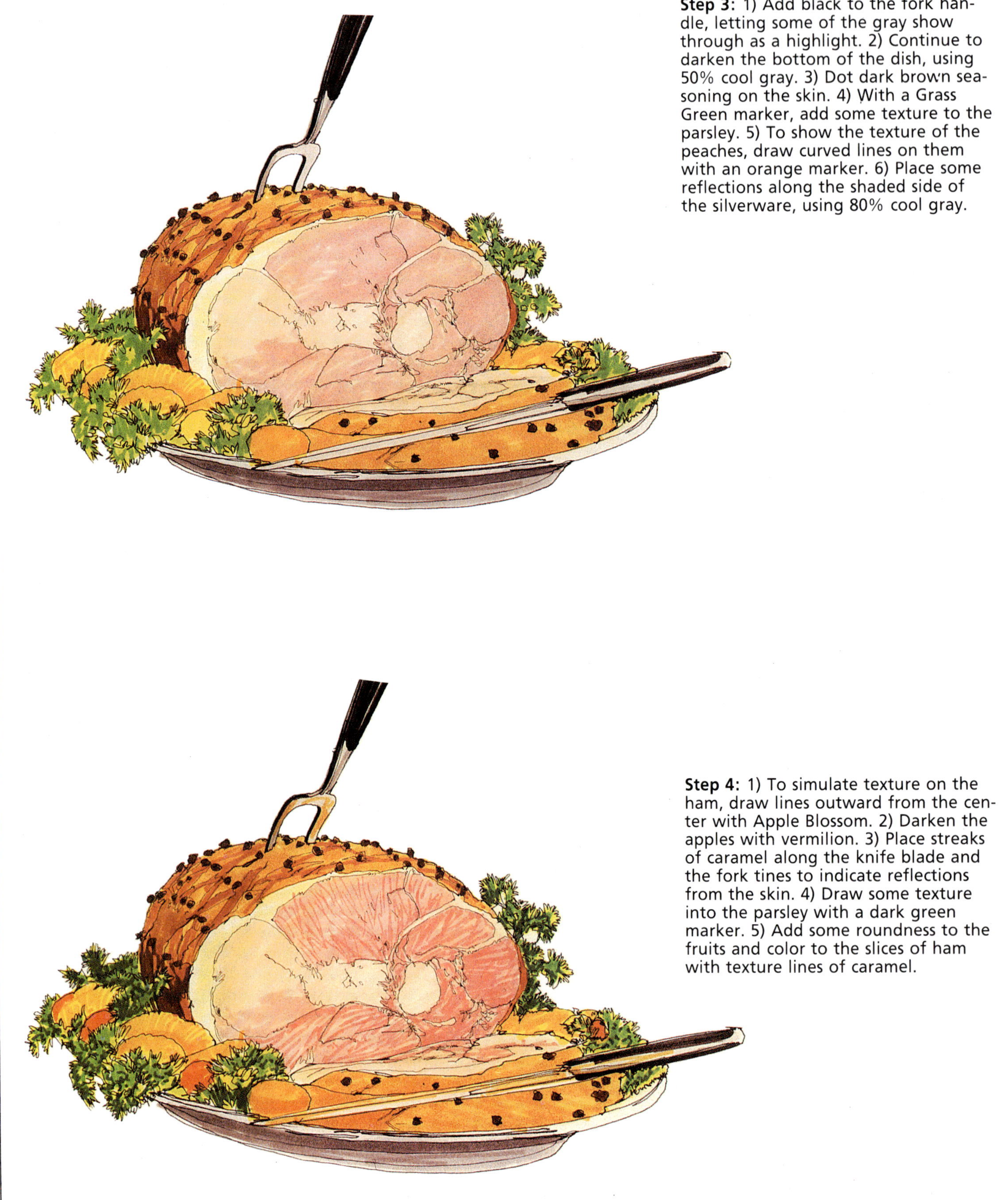

Step 3: 1) Add black to the fork handle, letting some of the gray show through as a highlight. 2) Continue to darken the bottom of the dish, using 50% cool gray. 3) Dot dark brown seasoning on the skin. 4) With a Grass Green marker, add some texture to the parsley. 5) To show the texture of the peaches, draw curved lines on them with an orange marker. 6) Place some reflections along the shaded side of the silverware, using 80% cool gray.

Step 4: 1) To simulate texture on the ham, draw lines outward from the center with Apple Blossom. 2) Darken the apples with vermilion. 3) Place streaks of caramel along the knife blade and the fork tines to indicate reflections from the skin. 4) Draw some texture into the parsley with a dark green marker. 5) Add some roundness to the fruits and color to the slices of ham with texture lines of caramel.

Step 5: 1) Heighten the ham's redness with texturizing strokes of blush. Keep this tone away from the fat and the middle bone. 2) Directly below the top of the plate, strengthen the shadow with 80% cool gray. 3) Using a No. 4 sable brush and Dr. Martin's bleed-proof white paint, add sharp highlights to the tops of the silverware. 4) With a broad nib, fill in the background with violet, making sure it doesn't bleed into the food, silverware, or plate. 5) When that layer of color dries, start at the horizon line and cover the violet with Indigo blue. Use a fine point around the food and silverware, then switch to a broad nib for the larger areas.

PROJECT 1: *FINISHED ART*

PROJECT 2: *FINISHED ART*

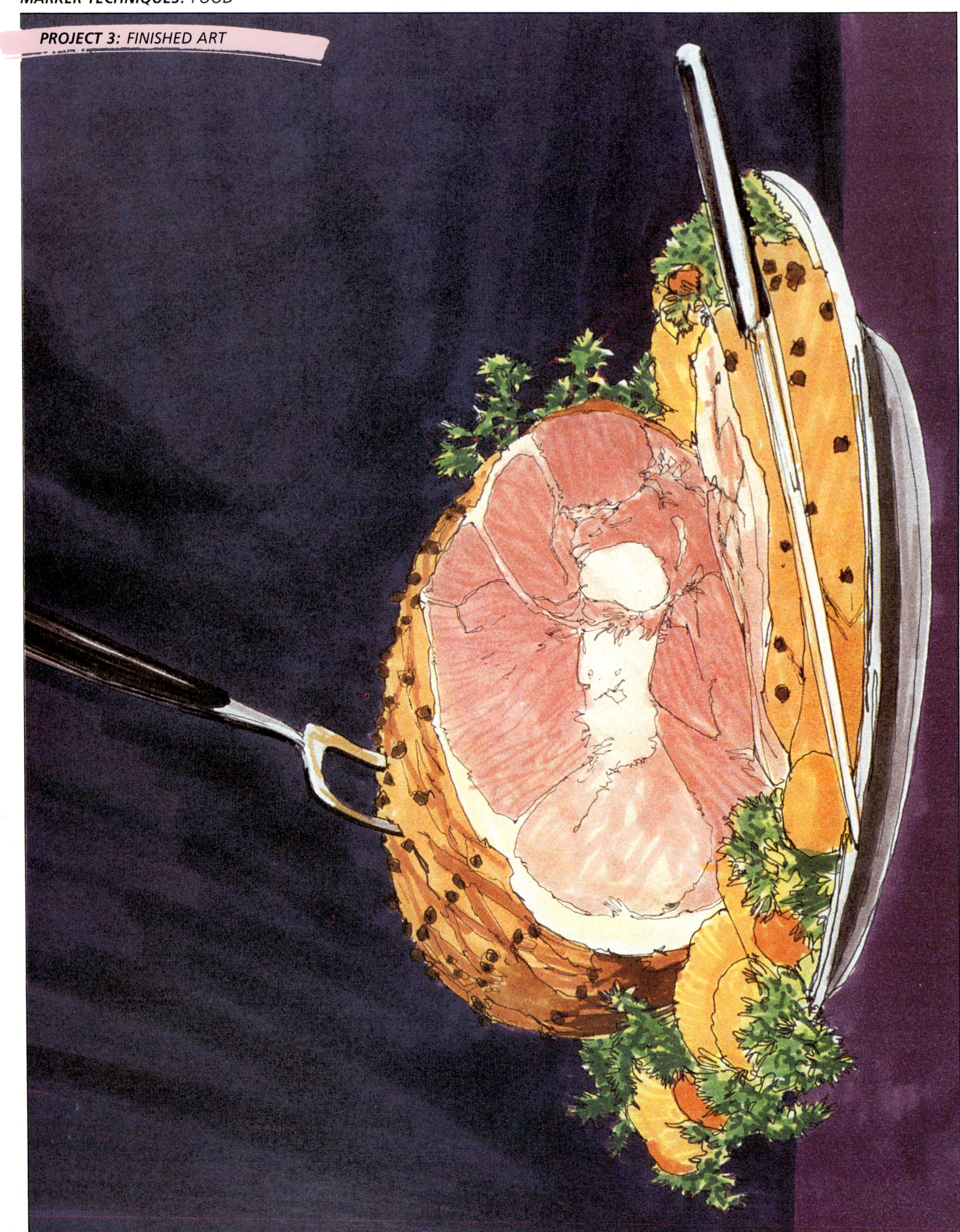

Please Tell Us

You bought *Marker Techniques: Food,* Workbook 7, because you wanted to learn how to use a new medium or improve your existing skills. We'd like to know how well this workbook has helped you do that. Complete this postage-paid form *after* you've finished the projects, fold it in *thirds,* staple it closed, and return it to us. *Your* opinion is important to us.

1) On a scale of 0 to 5 (0 = none and 5 = advanced) how much knowledge of the medium did you have before you started this workbook? _______

2) On a scale of 0 to 5 (0 = none and 5 = a lot) how much *more* do you know about the medium since you've completed this workbook? _______

3) Why did you choose this workbook in the series? ________________________________

____

4) Circle all the other workbooks in the series which you've completed. 1 2 3 4 5 6 8

5) If you haven't already, will you buy another workbook in the series? ____ yes ____ no,

because ____

6) What other medium(s) would you buy a workbook on? ____________________________

7) Did the artwork on the cover influence your decision to buy? ____ yes, because _________

____

no, because ____

____

8) Did we provide enough projects to keep you interested? ____ yes ____ no   To keep you challenged? ____ yes ____no

9) Would you have learned more quickly if there were more step-by-step illustrations in each project and shorter captions? ____ yes ____ no, because _____________________________

____

10) Did you like having practice paper provided? ____ yes ____ no ____ didn't make a difference. Did we provide ____ too few ____ enough ____ too many practice pages?

11) On a scale of 1 to 5 (1 = poor and 5 = excellent) please score the overall quality of the instruction. _______

Name ____

Address ____

City ___________________________ State ___________________________ Zip Code _________

Telephone ____

Occupation ____

BUSINESS REPLY MAIL

FIRST CLASS   PERMIT NO. 17   CINCINNATI, OHIO

POSTAGE WILL BE PAID BY ADDRESSEE

Graphic Art Book Editor
North Light Books
1507 Dana Avenue
Cincinnati, Ohio 45207

NO POSTAGE
NECESSARY
IF MAILED
IN THE
UNITED STATES

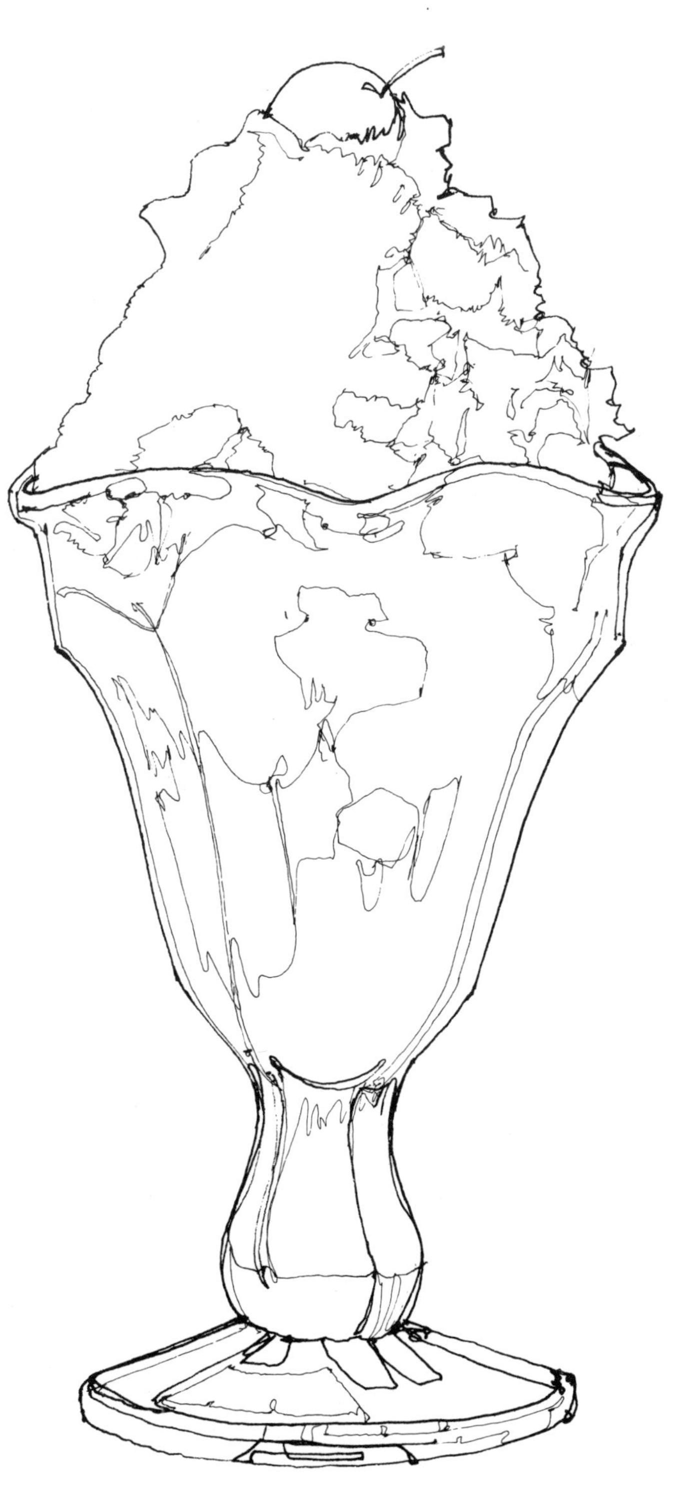

PROJECT 1: *PRACTICE*

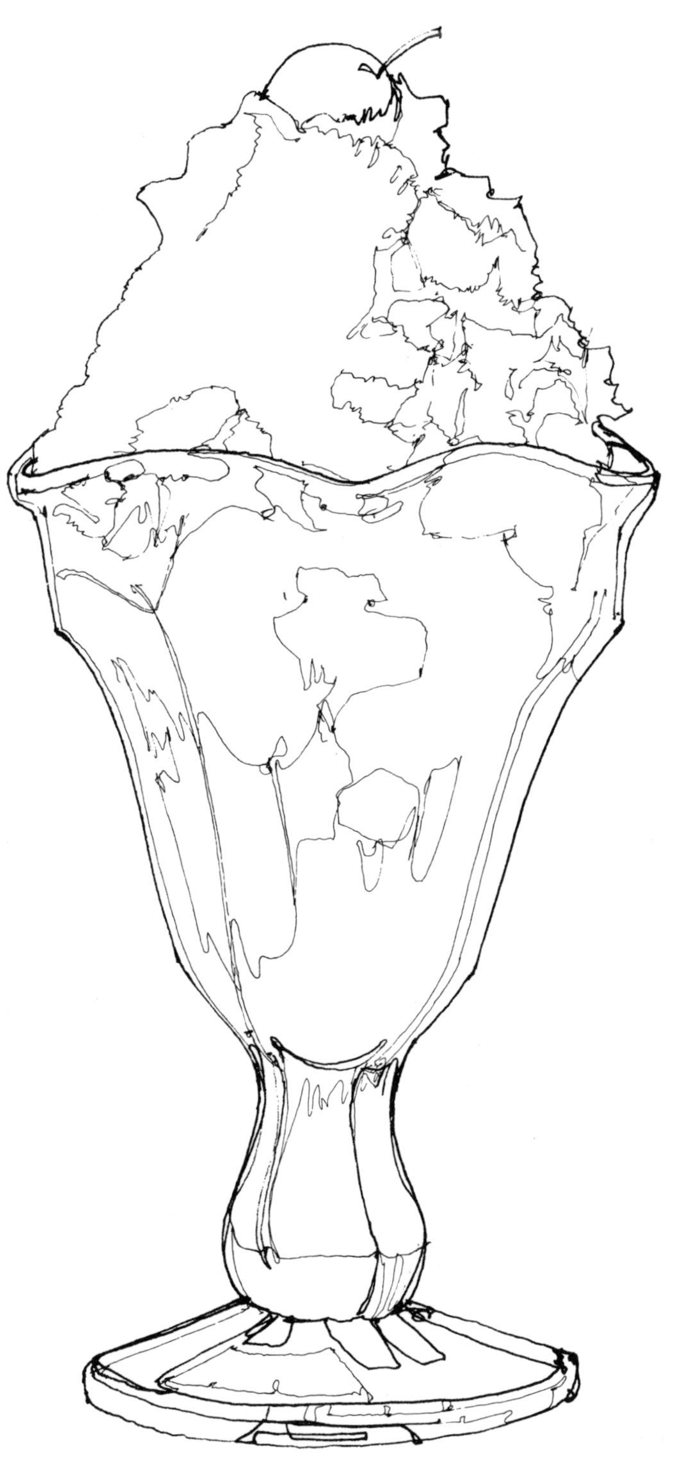

PROJECT 1: PRACTICE

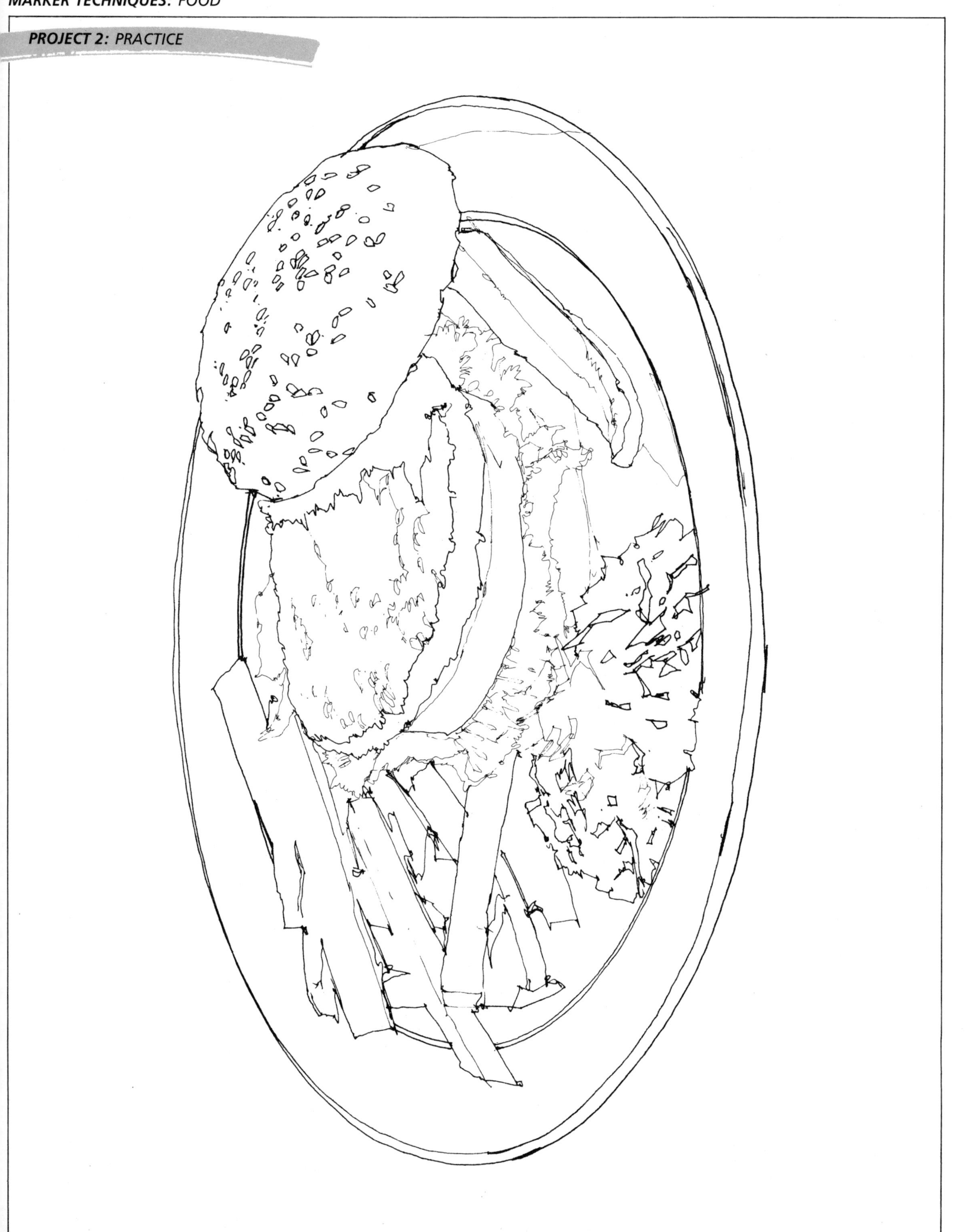

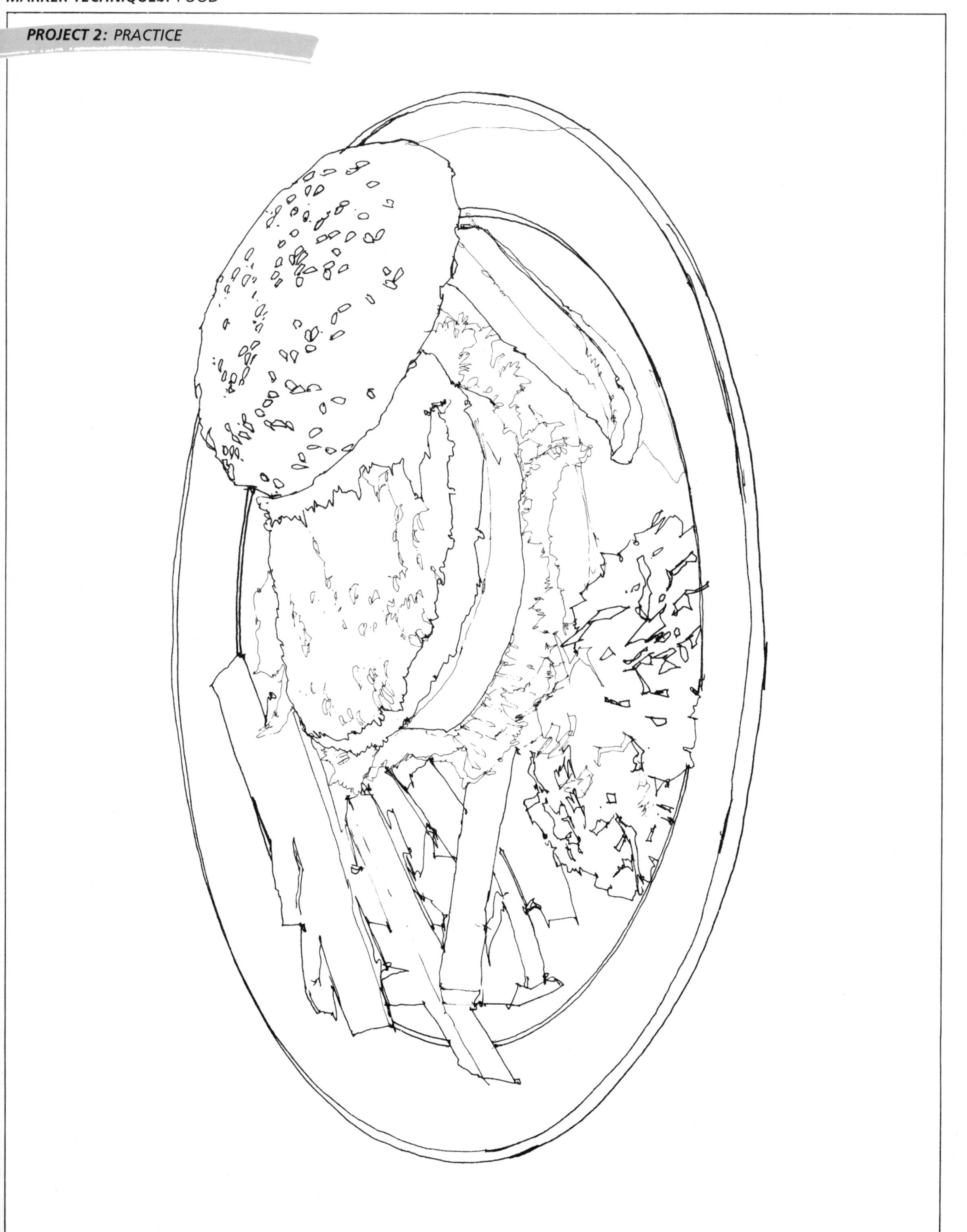

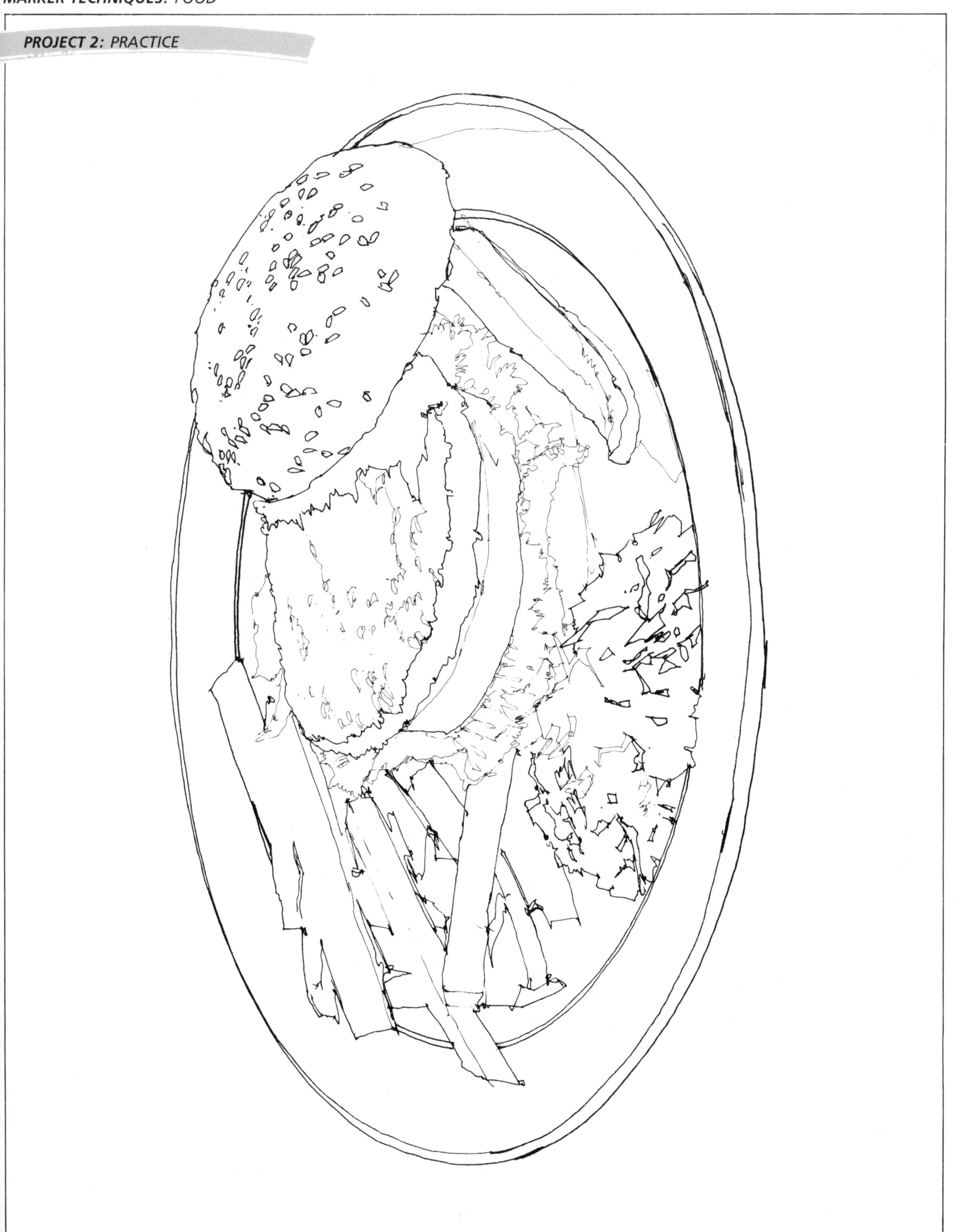

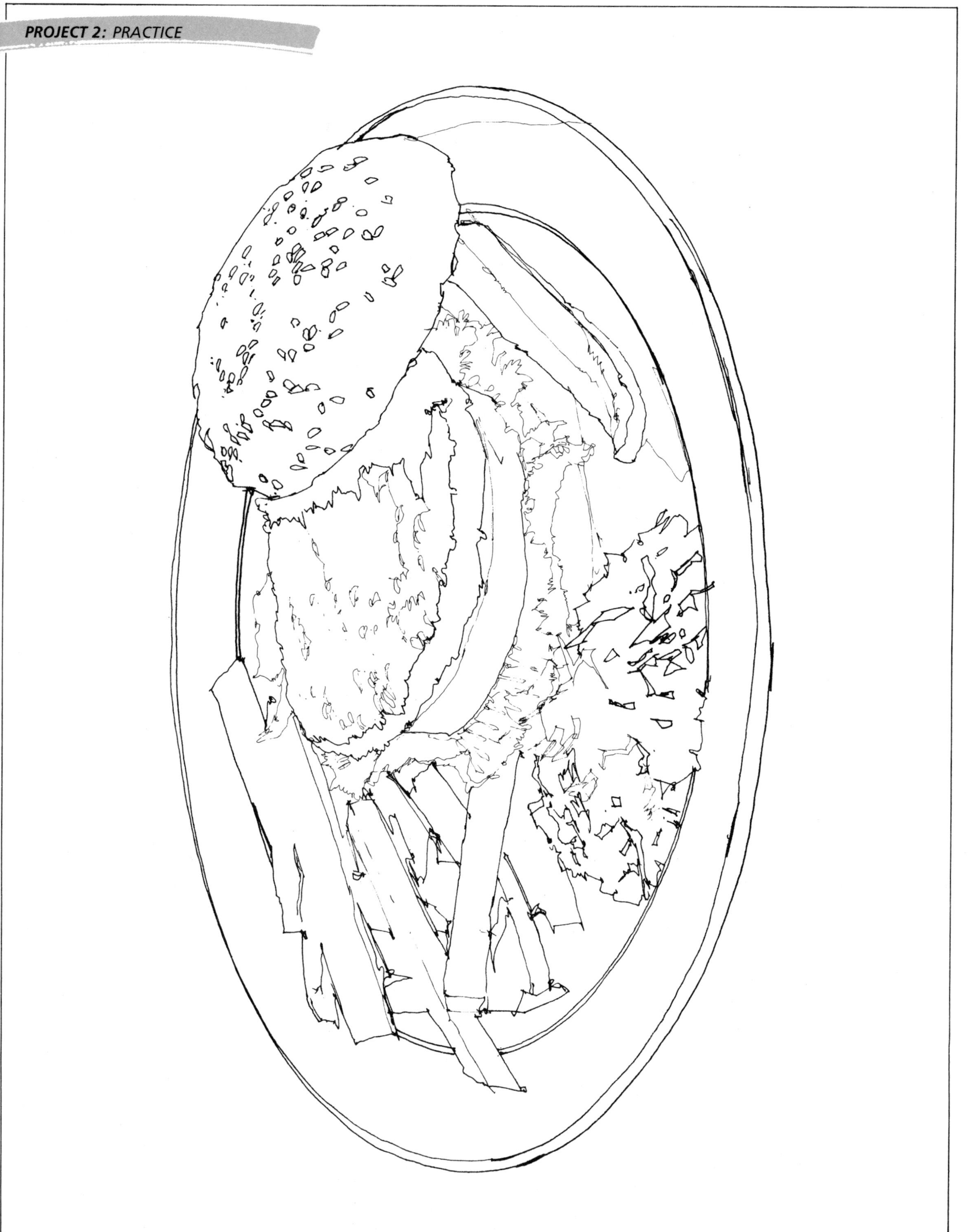

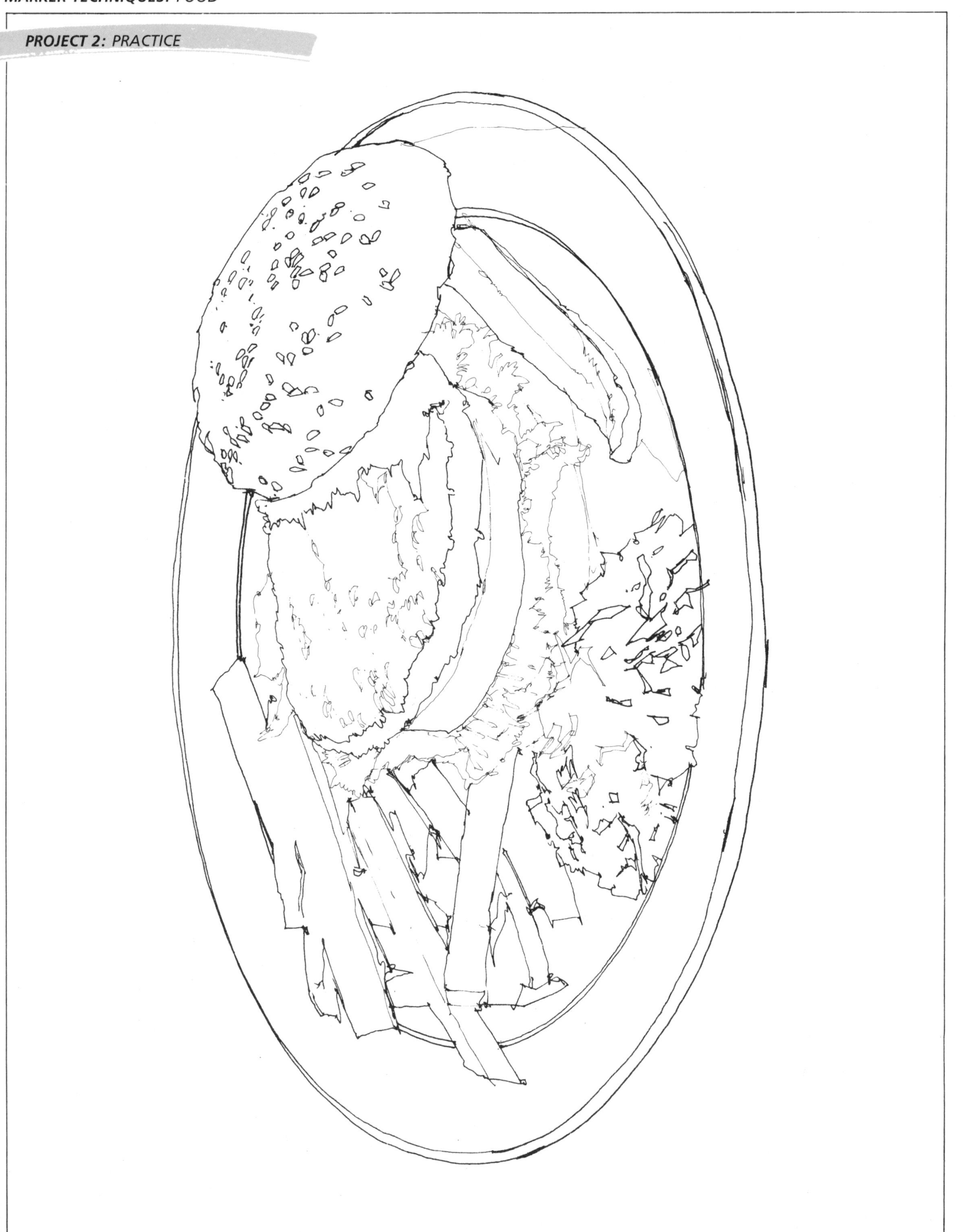

PROJECT 3: *PRACTICE*

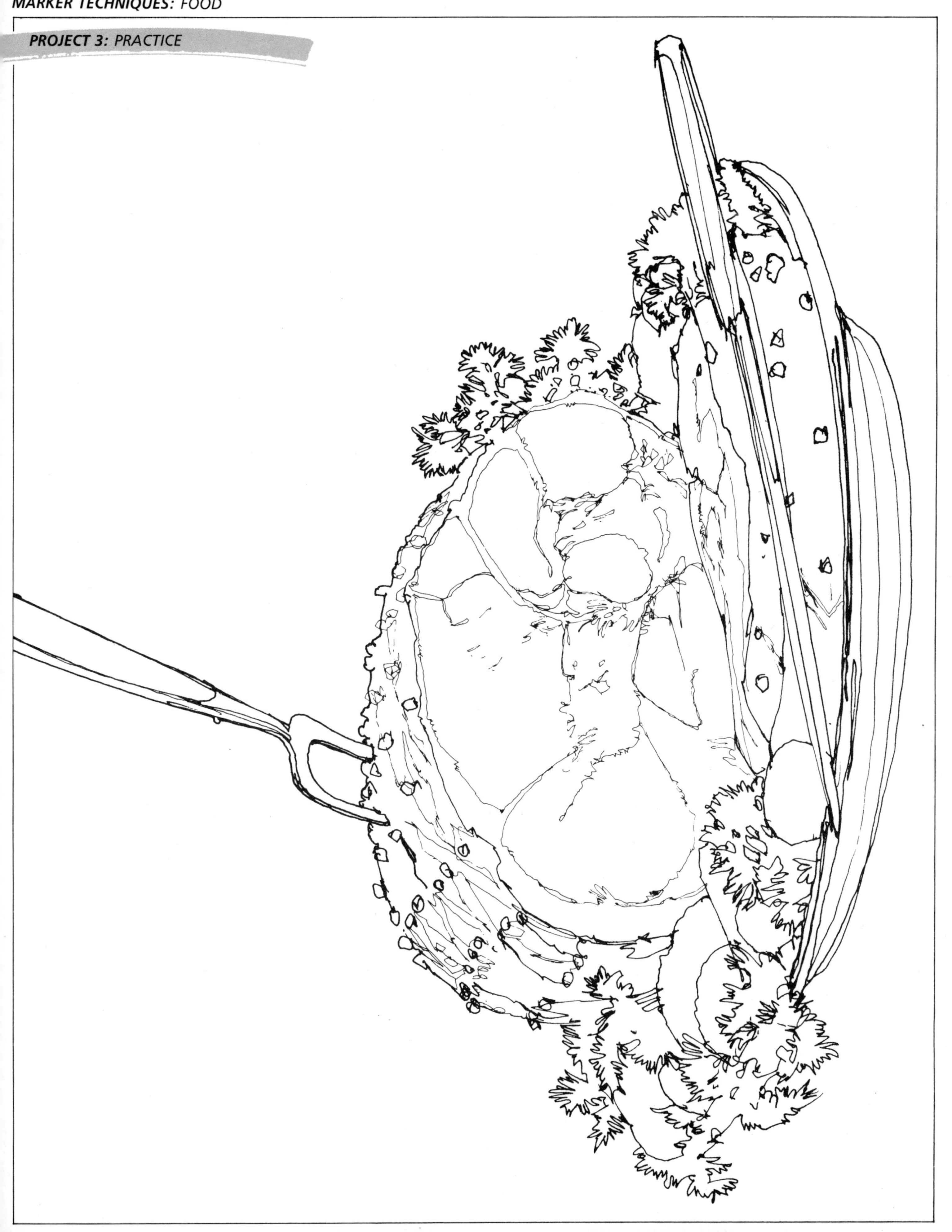

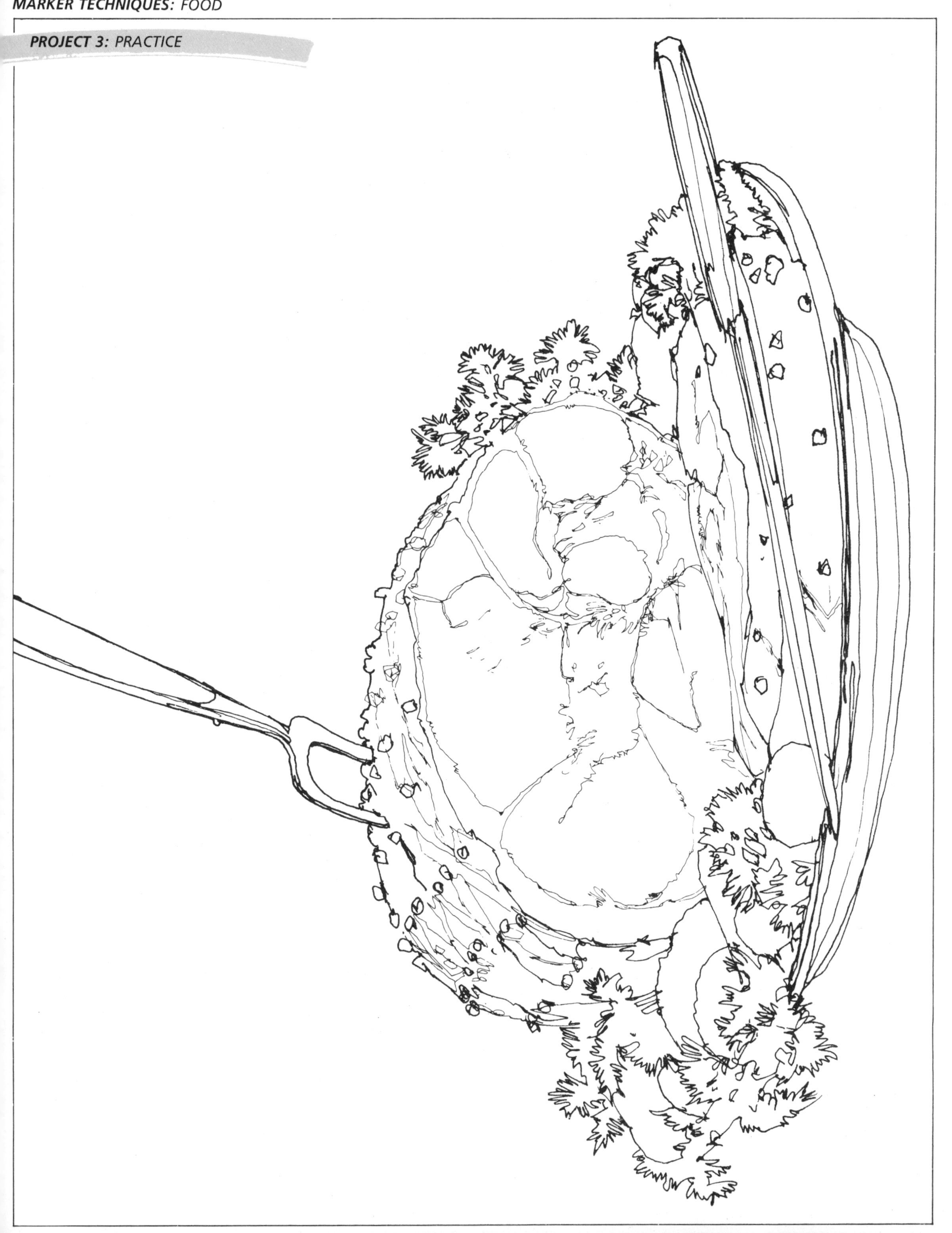

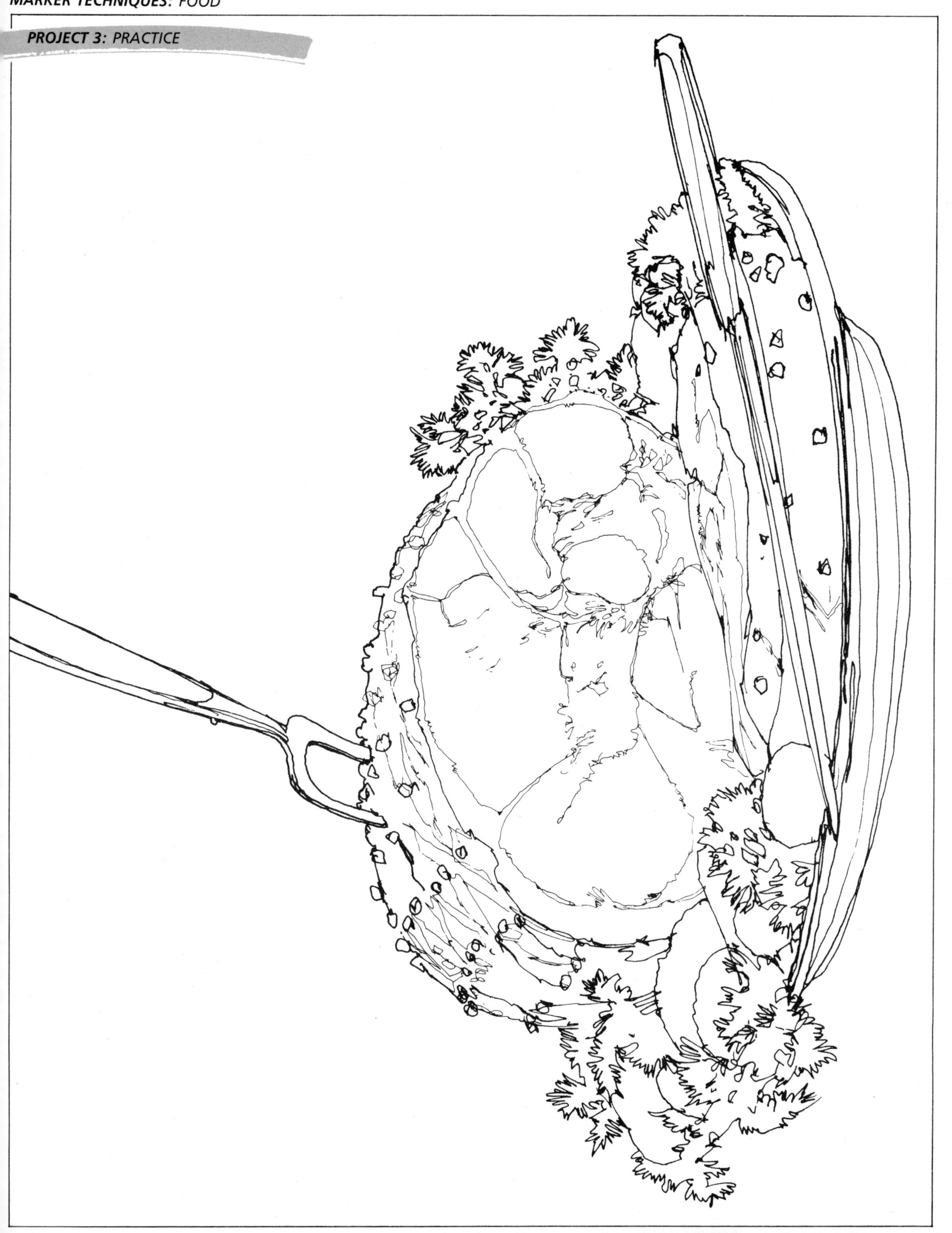

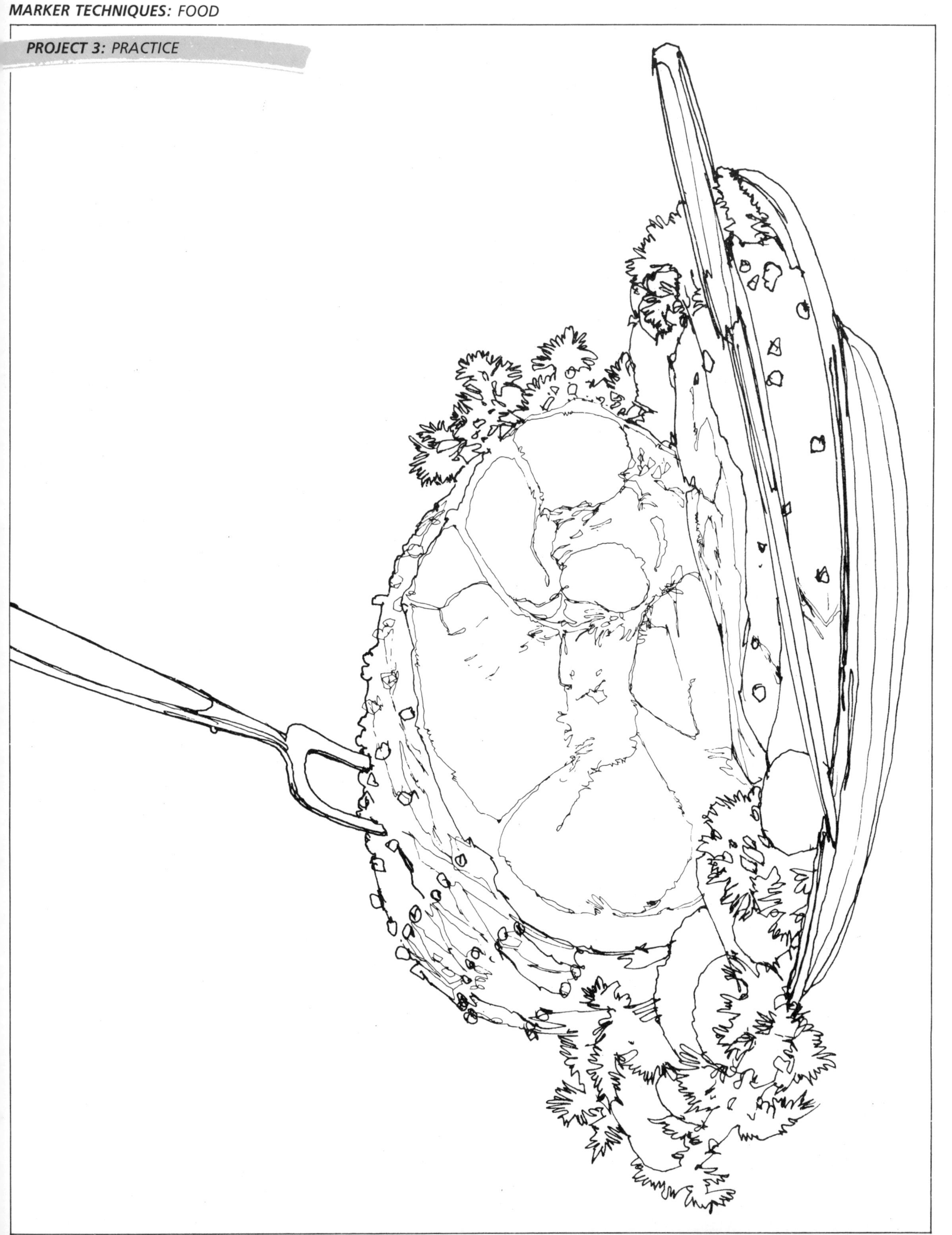